TUBAS

by Bob Temple

JUV
780.98
TEM

Published by The Child's World®
1980 Lookout Drive • Mankato, MN 56003-1705
800-599-READ • www.childsworld.com

Design element: Vector memory/Shutterstock.com
Photo credits: 13_Phunkod/Shutterstock.com: 4; Bildagentur Zoonar GmbH/Shutterstock.com: 14;
Chromakey/Shutterstock.com: 21 (French horn and trombone); Gau Meo/Shutterstock.com: 17;
Horatiu Bota/Shutterstock.com: 21 (flügelhorn and pocket trumpet); Igor Bulgarin/Shutterstock.
com: 7; kanashe_yuliya/Shutterstock.com: cover, 1; Monkey Business Images/Shutterstock.com:
18; Mr. Tobin/Shutterstock.com: 12; rustycanuck/Shutterstock.com: 8; Sashkin/Shutterstock.com:
21 (bugle); Walter Bilotta/Shutterstock.com: 21 (trumpet); Zhorov Igor/Shutterstock.com: 11

ISBN: 9781503831940
LCCN: 2018960416

Printed in the United States of America
PA02417

Table *of* Contents

CHAPTER ONE

The Tuba

As you sit and enjoy the orchestra's music, you hear a sound lower than all the others. Near the back of the group, you see musicians holding large, heavy-looking instruments. These are the instruments making the low sounds. What are these strange instruments? They're tubas!

❮ *These tubas are being played during an outdoor concert.*

CHAPTER TWO

Brass Instruments

There are many different types of instruments. **Wind instruments** make a sound when you air blow into them. **Brass instruments** are wind instruments made of metal. On most brass instruments, you can change the sound by pressing down on different buttons, or **valves**. Tubas are brass instruments. So are trumpets and French horns.

The tuba has the lowest sound of all the brass instruments.

Where are the wind instruments in this orchestra? Where are the brass instruments? ❯

CHAPTER THREE

How Old Are Tubas?

Tubas were invented so that brass bands would have a low-sounding, or **bass**, instrument. The first tuba was produced in 1835. Soon, tubas were being made in a variety of shapes and sizes. Each of these tubas was given a different name. Sousaphones and baritones are two popular kinds of tuba.

A tuba player is called a tubist or a tubaist.

❬ *This girl is playing a baritone.*

CHAPTER FOUR

Parts of a Tuba

Tubas have three important parts. The **mouthpiece** is a small, cup-shaped piece at one end. You blow air into the mouthpiece to produce a sound. The air moves through a long, curved, tube-like body.

"Embouchure" (AHM-boo-shur) is the word for a musician's lips on a brass instrument.

The big mouthpiece goes a little above and a bit below the player's lips. ❯

Along the tube are the valves that change the sounds the tuba makes. At the far end, the tube opens into a wide **bell** where the air and the sound come out.

Some tubas have valves on the front. Others have valves close to the top.

❮ *This man is playing a euphonium (yoo-FOH-nee-um). It is also called a tenor tuba.*

CHAPTER FIVE

The Tuba's Shape

Tubas are huge instruments. If you straightened out its curved tube, a tuba would be 16 feet (5 m) long! When you play a tuba, you must wrap your hands—and sometimes your arms— around a tuba to hold it.

In Latin, tuba means "horn" or "trumpet."

❮ *Tubas weigh about 30 pounds (13.6 kg)!*

Sousaphones are the kind of tuba
you usually see in marching bands.
Their tubing forms a large circle
that wraps around the player's
shoulder and body. Resting the
tubing on one shoulder makes the
instrument easier to carry. On most
tubas, the bell points upward, but
on a sousaphone, it points to the front.

*Sousaphones
were invented
around 1893.*

*These sousaphone players are in a marching band.
They've put covers on the bells of their instruments.* ❯

CHAPTER SIX

How Do You Play a Tuba?

To play a tuba, you tightly press your lips together and hold them to the mouthpiece. Then you blow air into the mouthpiece, making your lips buzz, or **vibrate**. Pressing the valves makes the tuba play different sounds, or **notes**. Changing the shape of your lips changes the sound, too.

❮ *It takes a lot of air to play a tuba!*

Tubas are an important part of many orchestras and bands. Most orchestras have tubas and baritones. Marching bands usually have sousaphones. But whenever you hear that low OOM-PAH OOM-PAH sound, you can be sure it's being made by some type of tuba!

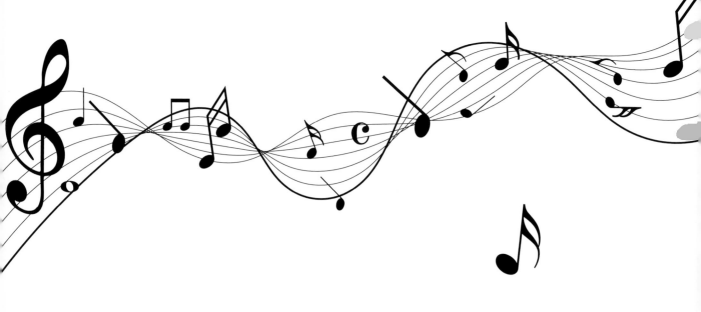

Other Brass Instruments

trumpet

pocket trumpet

bugle

flügelhorn

trombone

French horn

Glossary

bass (BAYSS) Bass is a deep or low sound. Tubas were invented to add a bass sound to brass bands.

bell (BELL) On a brass instrument, the bell is the wider end where the sound comes out. Tubas have a very large bell.

brass instruments (BRASS IN-struh-ments) Brass instruments are metal instruments that you play by blowing air through them and pressing valves to change the sound. Tubas are brass instruments.

mouthpiece (MOWTH-peece) On a brass instrument, the mouthpiece is the place where you put your mouth to play. Tubas have a large, cup-shaped mouthpiece.

notes (NOHTS) Notes are musical sounds. On tubas, you produce different notes by pressing the valves.

valves (VALVZ) On a brass instrument, valves are buttons you press to change the sound. Tubas have valves.

vibrate (VY-brayt) When something vibrates, it moves back and forth very quickly. To play a tuba, you vibrate your lips against the mouthpiece as you blow into it.

wind instruments (WIND IN-struh-ments) Wind instruments are instruments that produce a sound when you blow air through them. Tubas are wind instruments.

To Learn More

IN THE LIBRARY

Bechdolt, Jack. *Little Boy with a Big Horn*.
New York, NY: Golden Books, 2008.

Ganeri, Anita. *Brass Instruments*.
Mankato, MN: Smart Apple Media, 2012 .

Nunn, Daniel. *Brass.* Chicago, IL: Heinemann Library, 2012.

ON THE WEB

Visit our website for links about tubas:

childsworld.com/links

Note to Parents, Teachers, and Librarians: We routinely verify our Web links to make sure they are safe and active sites. So encourage your readers to check them out!

Index

About the Author

Bob Temple is the author of dozens of nonfiction books for children and young adults. He is also an award-winning journalist. Bob enjoys traveling, playing golf, and spending time with his wife and three adult children. Bob lives in Minnesota.